THE

MORAL SAYINGS

OF

PUBLIUS SYRUS,

A ROMAN SLAVE

THE

MORAL SAYINGS

OF

PUBLIUS SYRUS,

A ROMAN SLAVE.

PUBLIUS SYRUS

TRANSLATED BY

D. LYMAN

GYAN

Published by

GYAN

Gyan Publishing House
5, Ansari Road
Daryaganj, New Delhi-110002
Phone: 011-47034999, 9811692060
E-mail: books@gyanbooks.com

Distribution Network
gyanbooks.com
India, USA, Canada, UK, Australia

ISBN: 978-93-6208-056-1 (PB)
First Published, 1856

2nd Impression 2024

Printed at: Gyan Press, Delhi.

THE MORAL SAYINGS OF PUBLIUS SYRUS, A ROMAN SLAVE
Author: PUBLIUS SYRUS, Translator: D. LYMAN

THE

MORAL SAYINGS

OF

PUBLIUS SYRUS,

A ROMAN SLAVE.

From the Latin.

BY D. LYMAN, JR., A.M.

"A WORD FITLY SPOKEN IS LIKE APPLES OF GOLD IN PICTURES OF SILVER."

NEW YORK:
PUBLISHED BY ANDREW J. GRAHAM,
274 CANAL STREET (NEAR BROADWAY).

PREFACE.

When the Edinburgh Review was established, the following motto was proposed for it:

"*Tenui musam meditamur avenâ,*"

which Sydney Smith thus wittily renders: "we cultivate literature upon a little oatmeal." "But, says Smith, this was too near the truth to be admitted, and so we took our present grave motto from *Publius Syrus*, of whom none of us, I am sure, had ever read a single line." The motto adopted to which he refers, reads as follows:

"*Judex damnatur, cum nocens absolvitur.*"

"The judge is condemned, when the criminal is acquitted."

This sentiment perhaps expressed the purpose of the Reviewers better than any other that could have been found — which was to bring to the trial of the public judgment, certain institutions of England, which if but once put on trial would most surely be condemned. Years since, I sought in vain for a copy of the work from which that motto was drawn, and when later I learned from the above statement of Smith, that neither Jeffrey, Murray, Brougham, nor himself, had read a single line of Publius Syrus, I was surprised to discover what a reputation for learning and extensive erudition a man might acquire by an apt quotation from an inaccessible author. When still later a copy of Syrus came into my hands, it seemed strange that a writer of such wit and acuteness should not have been a great favorite with each of the Reviewers. That he was not, I could only account for by supposing that the original was seldom published by itself on account of its brevity; and that it was rarely translated, from the fact that many of the sayings derive their pith from the circumstance of their illustrating the character of personages represented in a play. But whether the Edinburgh Reviewers knew much or little of Syrus, matters not. A writer whom these Reviewers had never read, who yet furnished their journal with a very appropriate motto, and with whom many of our popular proverbs originated, I here take the liberty to introduce to the people in a free English dress, knowing that if his noble shade is yet cognizant of his literary remains, he will thank me for bringing him before a public more capable of appreciating his good things than a Roman mob, and better able to practice his wiser moral precepts if so disposed, than most of the best of his contemporaries.

I would only bespeak the charity of the reader for the seeming insipidity to be found in some of the Sayings. As these were gleaned, after Syrus's day, from his Mimes or Plays, the compiler of them would be liable to such a mistake as he might make who should attempt to gather from the works of our great English dramatist a complete list of Shakspeare proverbs; that is, he would be likely to insert in his collection, many sayings which would be without meaning, except when taken in the proper connection of the play — and many maxims of doubtful morality, because originally fitted to the mouth of a Shylock, or an Iago.

TRANSLATOR.

SKETCH OF THE LIFE OF SYRUS.

FROM THE FRENCH OF TH. BAUDEMENT.

TIME has wrought Syrus a singular destiny, building up for him a second reputation on the ruins of a first. Of his plays, which were the admiration of the Romans, the ages have brought down to us only a few sayings which were dispersed through them. The sayings were for that age of secondary consideration; they are now his chief performance. Thus deprived of the glory he once had, he has conquered another, and the once celebrated dramatist has become posterity's famous gnomic poet.

Like Terence and Phaedrus, Syrus passed his early years in slavery; but as we have no evidence that he was born a slave, it is supposed he became one, when Syria, his native country, was reduced to a Roman province by Pompey (year of Rome 690; B. C. 64). He was brought to Rome when about twelve years of age, by an inferior officer of the army, called Domitius, as report goes, and thereupon received the name *Syrus*, in accordance with the custom by which slaves took a name derived from that of their province. The young Syrian was fair, and well formed, of lively wit, and ready at repartee. Domitius taking him one day to the house of his patron to pay his court, as was a client's duty, the latter was struck with the elegance of his manners, and the beauty of his person — "an excellent recommendation," as Syrus himself has said, and particularly at Rome. The patron begged his little slave of Domitius, and the present was of course immediately made.

Syrus soon surprised his new master with sallies of wit superior to his age and condition. They were one day crossing a court together, in which a slave afflicted with the dropsy lay idly basking in the sun. "What are you doing there?" cried the master in an angry tone. "He is only warming his water," said Syrus; and the master's anger vanished in a laugh. On another occasion, his guests were discussing this question at table: what renders repose insupportable? The guests debated at great length without any prospect of agreement. The young slave had the audacity to throw in these words: "The feet of a gouty man;" sure of a pardon for his license from the patness of the remark—and the question was solved. On another occasion, pointing to an envious character who appeared that day more gloomy than usual—"Some misfortune, said he, has happened to that man, or some good fortune to some one else."

The master of Syrus desired that a liberal education should grace such rare faculties, and accordingly gave him one. He afterwards added the gift of liberty, a kindness which Syrus never forgot, which substituted for the bonds of servitude, ties dearer to both. "An affectionate freedman, said Syrus, is a son acquired without the aid of nature." At this period of his life it was, that according to the custom of freedmen, he took the name *Publius,* which was doubtless the surname of his master. It has been long maintained by some, but without proof, that he received it much later in life, from the favor of the people.

Hardly had Syrus received his freedom, when he visited Italy, and there gave himself up to the composition of Mimes, a kind of theatrical exhibition at that time very popular. This species of drama must not be confounded with pantomime, in which dancing and gesture represented only a series of disconnected pictures, for Ovid informs us that his "Art of Love" was exhibited in this way; nor with the Greek Mimes, in which the sentiment uttered was of more importance than the performance of the actors. The Mimes of the Romans, from which dancing was gradually banished, consisted at first of burlesque attitudes, and gross and often licentious farces, a species of exhibition more to the taste of the rabble than the regular Greek Mime, and better adapted besides to representation in theaters which admitted eighty thousand spectators.

As it was the chief purpose of the Mimes to raise a laugh, they were used to represent the failings and eccentricities of the higher classes, and the vulgar language and solecisms of the lower. Good imitation was therefore their perfection, and they were so pleasing to the Romans, that even in funeral processions, a band of mimics performed beside the chief mourners, whose leader (*Archimimus*) imitated the voice and gestures of the deceased.

Emboldened by success, they soon began to act little scenes which had no connection with each other, it is true, but in which the author himself performed the principal part, and in which each of the other actors, who played barefoot, added to his part whatever his own genius might suggest. As there could be no *final scene* in a play without plot, whenever an actor could not carry out his part, he took to his heels, and his flight put an end to the play.

The mimetic art was in this condition, that is to say, in its infancy, when Syrus composed his mimes. Laberius, a Roman knight, had just produced the first examples of mimetic poetry. Though aiming to amuse the people, he desired to instruct them, and therefore sought to blend useful truths and noble maxims with the pleasantries demanded in this species of comedy. He made the theater a school of morals, and a vehicle of political satire; and although he did not perform in his own pieces from a regard to his rank, he sprinkled them with biting epigrams designed to hit the all-powerful Cæsar.

Syrus followed him closely in this new path. He tempered the license of the mimes with many grave features, and a morality so severe, that Sėneca, in his disquisitions on the Stoic philosophy, often cited their maxims as authority, and still more frequently made them the themes of lengthy essays.

Syrus traveled Italy for a long time, writing and playing by turns, every where applauded as a poet and as an actor. The fame of his success finally reached Rome, and an occasion offered for his appearance there with honor to himself. When Cæsar was elected dictator a second time, he resolved to give the enslaved Romans such shows and amusements as should surpass in splendor and duration every thing they had before seen. Many days were to be devoted to games, to contests of all kinds, to theatrical representations in all quarters of the city, and in all languages of the then known world; conquered kings were to take part in them. To add to the success and splendor of the performances, Cæsar had solicited the presence of the most celebrated writers and actors, and among others, called Syrus to Rome. The news of the exhibitions attracted such multitudes from the neighboring provinces, that, as the houses were full, it was necessary to pitch tents for them in the streets and open fields; and many citizens, among the rest two senators, were crushed to death by the crowd.

Quite proud of his provincial success, when Syrus arrived in Rome, he had the courage to challenge to a trial of wits all the poets who adorned the stage. Every one accepted the challenge, and they were every one beaten. The caprice of Cæsar brought out against him, however, a formidable competitor. The dictator had commanded Laberius, then sixty years of age, to perform in one of his own mimes, which was a disgrace for a freeman, and above all for a knight. Laberius submitted, but his vengeance was at hand. The day and hour of the contest came. Cæsar was the judge, and all the senators and magistrates were its spectators, together with the whole order of knights, all the generals of the victorious army, all the strangers whom conquest or curiosity had made the guests of Rome, and last of all the people, that people whose highest desires were now comprised in bread and public shows —*panem et circenses.*

Laberius appeared on the stage, and began, in an admirable prologue, with deploring his compulsory appearance, as an actor, so little in keeping with his age and rank. "Behold me, then, who after having spent a life of sixty years without a stain on my honor, have left my house a knight, to return to it a mere actor. I have lived too long by one day." Then thinking of the talent of his young rival, and fearing a defeat, he added, to extenuate its possible disgrace, and gain the pity of the spectators — "what do I bring upon the stage to day? I have lost every thing — beauty of form, grace of mien, energy of expression, and the advantage of a good utterance. Like a tomb, I bear on my person only a name." But he soon recovered his self-possession, and in his performance launched against tyranny a torrent of severe invective, the application of which was readily seen. Thus acting the part of a slave, escaping from the hands of his executioner, he fled shouting — "It is all over with us, Romans, liberty is lost!" "He who becomes a terror to multitudes, he added a moment after, has multitudes to dread"— while his gaze was continually fixed on the impassible dictator.

The performance ended, Cæsar invited the audacious actor to take a seat among the spectators of his own rank. Syrus, whose turn to perform had now come, then approaching Laberius, said with a modest air, "be so good as to receive with kindness as a spectator, him against whom you have contended as an actor." Laberius sought a place among the ranks of the knights, who however crowded together so as not to allow him a seat. Cicero, who was somewhat given to raillery, shouted to him from a distance, directing his irony at once against the actor and the new batch of senators: "I would cheerfully give you my place, if it were not too much crowded." "I am astonished," pertly replied Laberius, "to hear that from a man who is wont to sit so well on two seats at once;" a witty allusion to the equivocal character of the orator, a friend at the same time of Cæsar and Pompey. He seated himself as he best could, to listen to his rival.

Syrus at length appeared, the crowd shouting their applause, and played the piece he had composed; but we are ignorant even of its title.

Whether from resentment, or a sense of justice, Cæsar awarding to Syrus the prize of the theatrical contest, immediately passed him the triumphal palm, saying to the knight, with a mocking smile, "Although I was on your side, Laberius, a Syrian has beaten you." "Such is the fate of man," answered the poet; "to-day, every thing; to-morrow, nothing." Notwithstanding, to restore the honor of the knight, lost by compliance with his own orders, Cæsar passed him a gold ring, the symbol of knightly rank, and added to it a present of five hundred thousand sesterces (about nineteen thousand dollars).

This solemn contest between the two greatest mime writers of Rome, was not the last; it was sometimes repeated. But Laberius, thenceforward confessing the superiority of his conqueror, was content with saying, that another would some day claim it over him; while Cæsar, according to Aulus Gellius, continued to prefer Syrus. After the death of his rival, and notwithstanding his jealous predictions, Syrus reigned sole master of the stage for nearly fifteen years,—*Romae scenam tenet*, says St. Jerome in his chronicle; and he continued sole master of it during the rest of his life, which was prolonged, as is generally supposed, to the beginning of the reign of Augustus (year of Rome 725; B. C. 29).

Many testimonials of the ancients prove that the renown of this writer did by no means die with him, and St. Jerome informs us, that after the lapse of four centuries, he was read by the Roman youth in the public schools. Seneca, the tragedian, borrowed from him more than once, and the philosopher often speaks in his praise. "He is," said he, "the most sublime of dramatic poets, when he abstains from the nothings designed for the lowest benches of the amphitheater." "How well, he writes on another occasion, would his sayings become, not the barefooted actors of mimes, but the buskined tragedian!"

Macrobins and Aulus Gellius, who with Seneca have done most to preserve us these sayings, are as loud in their praises of them as the philosopher. Petronius, who admired this author so much as to compare him with Cicero, grants the latter superiority in acquirements only: "Syrus," said he, "had the nobler soul." There is in fact nothing more elevated than the sentiments expressed in the greater part of these sayings, all that remains of the works of the poet, precious fragments snatched by science from the ravages of time. This little collection is, as it were, the storehouse of ancient ethics, and Seneca in his long essays has added nothing to them. The very form in which Syrus presented them, in the nervous conciseness of his iambics, must have been far more efficient in gaining men over to the practice of virtue, than all the arguments of the Stoic school. Marcus Agrippa, that illustrious contemporary of our poet, declared that a single saying had made him a good brother and a fast friend. Seneca, who has written so much on wisdom, has admitted how much she can gain by the neatness and brevity of poetic expression. "We discourse lengthily," said he, "to men on the contempt and use of riches, and the principles of morality, but the same precepts, clothed in verse, make a more vivid and lasting impression on the mind." To make such impressions in favor of virtue and morality was the glorious purpose which Syrus had in view

THE SAYINGS OF PUBLIUS SYRUS.

(FROM THE LATIN.)

1.

As men, we are all equal in the presence of death.

2.

The evil you do to others you may expect in return.

3.

Allay the anger of your friend by kindness.

4.

To dispute with a drunkard is to debate with an empty house.

5.

Receive an injury rather than do one.

6.

A trifling rumor may cause a great calamity.

7.

To do two things at once is to do neither.

8.

A hasty judgment is a first step to a recantation.

9.

Suspicion cleaves to the dark side of things.

10.

To love one's wife with too much passion, is to be an adulterer.

11.

Hard is it to correct the habit already formed.

12.

A small loan makes a debtor; a great one, an enemy.

13.

Age conceals the lascivious character; age also reveals it.

14.

Bitter for a free man is the bondage of debt.

15.

Even when we get what we wish, it is not ours.

16.

We are interested in others, when they are interested in us

17.

Every one excels in something in which another fails.

18.

Do not find your happiness in another's sorrow.

19.

An angry lover tells himself many lies.

20.

A lover, like a torch, burns the more fiercely the more agitated.

21.

Lovers know what they want, but not what they need.

22.

A lover's suspicions are a waking man's dreams.

23.

There is no penalty attached to a lover's oath.

24.

The anger of lovers renews the strength of love.

25.

A god could hardly love and be wise.

26.

Love is youth's privilege, but an old man's shame.

27.

If your parent is just, revere him; if not, bear with him.

28.

If you cannot bear the faults of a friend, you make them your own [because you have not the charity to correct them].

29.

Be not blind to a friend's faults, nor hate him for them.

30.

If you bear the faults of a friend, you make them your own [that is, you show a disposition to correct them].

31.

When you fall short in what is due to yourself, you are lacking towards your friends.

32.

Friendship either finds or makes equals.

33.

Friendship ever profits, but love ever injures.

34.

Confidence is the only bond of friendship.

35.

Adversity shows whether we have friends, or only the shadows of friends.

36.

We should not injure a friend even in sport.

37.

The loss of a friend is the greatest of losses.

38.

The loss which is unknown is no loss at all.

39.

Love cannot be stifled, but it may die out.

40.

There can be no alliance between Love and Fear.

41.

Love is the source of an idle anxiety.

42.

Love, like a tear, rises in the eye and falls upon the breast.

43.

Time, not the will, can put an end to love.

44.

Love's wounds are cured by their cause.

45.

The will controls the beginnings of love, but not its endings.

46.

We all seek to know whether we shall be rich; but no one ask whether he shall be good.

47.

The plainer the table, the more wholesome the food.

48.

We should not credit the utterances of an angry spirit.

49.

A wise man rules his passions, a fool obeys them.

50.

When reason rules, money is a blessing.

51.

Reason guides, and not the eye, when chaste women select a husband.

52.

A [haughty] spirit in disgrace is a show for the rabble.

53.

Human reason grows rich by self-conquest.

54.

To know when to fear, is to be in the path of safety.

55.

He has existed only, not lived, who lacks wisdom in old age.

56.

Death laughs when old women frolic.

57.

Woman becomes good, when she is openly wicked.

58.

When the tree has fallen, any one can cut wood.

59.

Tension weakens the bow; the want of it, the mind.

60.

Art avails nothing, when chance determines the issue.

61.

Keep a sharp watch where you would not lose.

62.

Excessive severity misses its own aim.

63.

Audacity augments courage; hesitation, fear.

64.

If you can not become a harper, become a piper.

65.

When Gold argues the cause, eloquence is impotent.

66.

Woman loves or hates: she knows no middle course.

67.

Concert of action renders slight aid efficient.

68.

What greater evil could you wish a miser, than long life?

69.

You can easily get the better of Avarice, if you are not avaricious yourself.

70.

Money does not sate Avarice, but stimulates it.

71.

No amount of gain satisfies Avarice.

72.

The [rich] miser suffers more from a loss than a [poor] sage.

73.

Avarice is the source of its own sorrows.

74.

The avaricious man's best deed is his death.

75.

Greediness ill-becomes any one; least of all, an old man.

76.

A well-planned project often turns out ill.

77.

He sleeps well, who knows not that he sleeps ill.

78.

It is well to yield up a pleasure, when a pain goes with it.

79.

The guilty man deserves to lose the money with which he would bribe the judge.

80.

Happy he who died when death was desirable.

81.

A good reputation is a second patrimony.

82.

We make the nearest approaches to the gods in our good deeds.

83.

No one but a knave or a fool thinks a good deed thrown away.

84.

The more benefits bestowed, the more received.

85.

Never forget a favor received; be quick to forget a favor bestowed.

86.

Gratitude is a spur for your benefactors.

87.

To receive a favor is to pawn your freedom.

88.

He who can not give, should not receive.

89.

To give to the deserving, is to lay all men under obligation.

90.

A gift in season is a double favor to the needy.

91.

He who boasts of a favor bestowed, would like it back again.

92.

Sympathy in benevolence is the closest of all kinships.

93.

A true benevolence knows the reason of its gifts.

94.

To die by another's command is to endure two deaths.

95.

A favor granted before it is asked, is doubly acceptable.

96.

Past happiness augments present wretchedness.

97.

He dies twice who perishes by his own hand.

98.

Aid rendered the wrong-doer, makes you the greater sinner.

99.

Conquest over one's self, in the hour of victory, is a double triumph.

100.

Multiply your acts of kindness, and you teach the recipient to return them.

101.

Venus yields to caresses, not to compulsion.

102.

Mercy shown [to the wretched] may become a bulwark of defense.

103.

Happy is the voyage that brings the good together.

104.

A good reputation, even in darkness, keeps on shining.

105.

A death that ends the [incurable] ills of life, is a blessing.

106.

Money is worth something when good sense disburses it.

107.

One man's happy hour is another's bitter time of trial.

108.

A good reputation is more valuable than money.

109.

We must master our good fortune, or it will master us.

110.

It is a happy disgrace that saves from a greater peril.

111.

The slothful enjoyment of it, is the worst part of prosperity.

112.

Even in death, a good man would not deceive.

113.

To spare the guilty is to injure the innocent.

114.

The more skillfully the language of goodness is assumed, the greater the depravity.

115.

A good man's severity is next neighbor to justice.

116.

A mean man's generosity is a generous man's meanness.

117.

A good man loves to sit at a good man's table.

118.

In the presence of a good man, anger is speedily cooled.

119.

It is well to moor your bark with two anchors.

120.

Learn to see in another's calamity the ills which you should avoid.

121.

The good which is prevented is not annihilated.

122.

The slower to kindle, the more terrible the wrath of a generous soul.

123.

The good man never coquets with iniquity.

124.

Life is short, but its ills make it seem long.

125.

The bare recollection of anger kindles anger.

126.

There is no sight in the eye, when the mind does not gaze.

127.

While teasing for horns, the camel lost his ears.

128.

He keeps furthest from danger who looks out while he is safe.

129.

A chaste wife rules her husband by deferring to his wishes.

130.

Misfortune sometimes visits him whom she has often passed by.

131.

Trust no man as a friend till you have tried him.

132.

Beware of him who has once deceived you.

133.

You can never dispense with prudence.

134.

The wounds of conscience always leave a scar.

135.

The danger despised is the first to reach us.

136.

Falsities are quick to appear in their true character.

137.

We are anxious to avoid the faults which we are ashamed to have committed.

138.

There is but a step between a proud man's glory and his disgrace.

139.

The joys of the worthless speedily turn to their own destruction.

140.

Oblivion is a guaranty against civil war.

141.

Make your beloved angry, if you wish him to love you.

142.

The request of a master is a command.

143.

An agreeable companion on a journey is as good as a carriage.

144.

Society in shipwreck is a comfort to all.

145.

Congeniality of disposition is the strongest of ties.

146.

Consult your conscience, rather than popular opinio

147.

Consider what you ought to say, and not what you think.

148.

You will gain your point better by moderation than anger.

149.

Many receive advice, few profit by it.

150.

We tolerate without rebuke the vices with which we have grown familiar.

151.

Man's most prudent counselor is time.

152.

Wisdom had rather be buffeted than not be listened to.

153.

Folly had rather be unheard than be buffeted.

154.

It is hard to touch that which brings pain by mere contact.

155.

A god can hardly disturb a man truly happy.

156.

Have courage, or cunning, when you deal with an enemy.

157.

It is folly to be too frank with impudent familiarity.

158.

Let fly many arrows, and no two will hit in the same place.

159.

He who longs for death, confesses that life is a failure.

160.

The sick man's intemperance makes the physician relentless.

161.

Reproach in misfortune is an unseasonable cruelty.

162.

It is barbarity, not courage, that can slay babes.

163.

Tears gratify a savage nature, they do not melt it.

164.

Anger blazes forth but once against its object.

165.

He who has no home, is a dead man without a sepulcher.

166.

He whom the popular voice approves, holds the key of the people's treasure.

167.

He who can get more than belongs to him, is apt to accommodate his desires to his opportunity.

168.

To be always giving, is to encourage a forcible taking when you refuse to give.

169.

Every man is a master in his own calling.

170.

Patience is a remedy for every sorrow.

171.

What happens to one man may happen to all.

172.

When the people detest a man's life, they call for his death.

173.

The greatest of comforts is to be free from blame.

174.

There is no safety in regaining the favor of an enemy.

175.

Anger and inordinate desire are the worst of counselors.

176.

To refuse when extreme necessity prays, is to condemn to death.

177.

The tongue of the condemned can speak, but cannot avert the doom.

178.

The gain acquired at the expense of reputation, should be counted a loss.

179.

There is rarely a loss where plenty is unknown.

180.

The blessing which could be received, can be taken away.

181.

It is enough to think ill of an enemy, without speaking it.

182.

You can find more friends at the tenth hour, than at the first.

183.

A homely woman is one of the most comely of apes.

184.

Wisdom is acquired by meditation.

185.

While we stop to think, we often miss our opportunity.

186.

Deliberation should be protracted, when the decision is to be final.

187.

When utility is our aim, a little delay is advisable.

188.

It is madness to put confidence in error.

189.

When Providence favors, you can make a safe voyage on a twig.

190.

The gods methinks must laugh when a prosperous man puts up a prayer [for more].

191.

Whatever you can lose, you should reckon of no account.

192.

It is easy for women to shed tears without salt.

193.

One day treats us like a hireling nurse, another, like a mother.

194.

Fear lest a day snatch away what a single day has acquired.

195.

It is hard to keep that which every one covets.

196.

Turn a deaf ear to calumnious reports.

197.

Yesterday should be the teacher of to-day.

198.

Discord gives a relish for concord.

199.

Reflect on every thing you hear, but believe only on proof.

200.

Preparations for war should be long in making, that victory may be the more speedy.

201.

Divide the fire, and you will the sooner put it out.

202.

Mental pain is harder to bear than corporeal.

203.

When pain cannot increase, it dies away.

204.

He who has prospered in life, should stay at home.

205.

The builder of a house should not leave it unfinished.

206.

The courage of the soldiers depends upon the wisdom of the general.

207.

Avoid the sweet which is like to become a bitter.

208.

The rewards of talent and fortune are offered to all.

209.

Pleasant is the remembrance of the ills that are past.

210.

When life passes agreeably is the best time to die.

211.

The more promptly bestowed, the greater the kindness.

212.

Avoid cupidity, and you conquer a kingdom.

213.

The less a mortal desires, the less he needs.

214.

How sad his fate, who grows old through anxiety.

215.

A kindness should be received in the spirit that prompted it.

216.

There is no need of spurs when the horse is running away.

217.

In place of giving an angry man arms, we should take them away.

218.

Speed itself is slow when cupidity waits.

219.

For him who loves labor, there is always something to do.

220.

It is a kingly spirit that can return good deeds for reproaches.

221.

An inglorious life is the next thing to death.

222.

Solitude is the mother of anxieties.

223.

The party to which the rabble belong is ever the worst.

224.

Even calamity becomes virtue's opportunity.

225.

The wretched reflect either too much or too little.

226.

Patience is affliction's haven.

227.

The good to which we have become accustomed, is often an evil.

228.

Even a single hair casts its shadow.

229.

Celerity is tardiness when ardent desire urges.

230.

He who takes counsel of good faith, is just even to an enemy.

231.

We should keep our word even to the undeserving.

232.

Pain will force even the truthful to speak falsely.

233.

It is sometimes expedient to forget who we are.

234.

We may with advantage at times forget what we know.

235.

Those who do injustice, hate it.

236.

Even when the wound is healed, the scar remains.

237.

Even when there is no law, there is conscience.

238.

The tyrant can hardly be said to hold even a doubtful sway.

239.

Pecuniary gain first suggested to men to make Fortune a goddess.

240.

The fiercer the contention, the more honorable the reconciliation.

241.

The hope of reward is the solace of labor.

242.

The wise man corrects his own errors by observing those of others.

243.

The further the fall, the greater the hurt.

244.

Depravity is revealed in outward action, but its source is within.

245.

The life which we live is but a small part of the real life.

246.

A great man may commence life in a hovel.

247.

He suffers exile who refuses to serve his country.

248.

Men will judge your past deeds by your last.

249.

Versatility of mind is a natural bias to folly.

250.

It is easier to add to a great reputation than to get it.

251.

Good fortune renders a man agreeable, if the good fortune is not seen.

252.

By concealing the deed, you render the accusation more serious.

253.

Calumny is a malevolent lie.

254.

Many consult their reputation; but few their conscience.

255.

The master is a slave when he fears those whom he rules.

256.

He confesses his crime who flees the tribunal.

257.

Prosperity is the nurse of ill temper.

258.

A prosperous worthlessness is the curse of high life.

259.

Endure the heavy burdens, and you will the more easily carry the lighter.

260.

Bear without murmuring what cannot be changed.

261.

Be patient under your afflictions, that you may be able to endure your happiness.

262.

You should hammer your iron when it is glowing hot.

263.

No one ever lost honor but him who never had any.

264.

He who has forfeited his honor can lose nothing more.

265.

What is left when honor is lost?

266.

Confidence, like life, never returns to him whom she has once left.

267.

A fair exterior is a silent recommendation.

268.

Fortune has no lawful control over men's morals.

269.

A great property is a great bondage for the owner.

270.

Fortune often spares men a present affliction, that they may suffer a greater.

271.

Fortune makes a fool of him whom she favors too much.

272.

Fortune masters us if we do not master her.

273.

Fortune has no more power over our destiny than our own actions.

274.

Fortune is not satisfied with inflicting one calamity.

275.

When Fortune is on our side, popular favor bears her company.

276.

Fortune has more power over a man than his own forethought.

277.

When fortune flatters, she does it to betray.

278.

When the edifice of our Fortune is but slightly fractured, a chasm opens through the whole.

279.

Fortune makes many loans, but gives no presents.

280.

Fortune is like glass; the brighter the glitter, the more easily broken.

281.

The great gifts of Fortune are waited on by fear.

282.

It is more easy to get a favor from Fortune, than to keep it.

283.

His own character is the arbiter of every one's fortune.

284.

It is a fraud to receive the trust which you cannot return.

285.

Put a bridle on your tongue, but at all hazards on your baser members.

286.

With but few, is a repetition of punishment remedial.

287.

Frugality is poverty disguised with a good name.

288.

Vain are his prayers who cannot grant a prayer.

289.

An over-taxed patience gives way to fierce anger.

290.

The future struggles that it may not become the past.

291.

Where there is no shame there is double the guilt.

292.

Groans show the pain, but do not remove it.

293.

A noble steed is not annoyed by the barking of dogs.

294.

The gladiator lays his plans after he enters the arena.

295.

The termination of a present is one step toward a future evil.

296.

It vexes a cheerful giver to meet with a scowling acceptance.

297.

A serious charge, even when mildly uttered, gives pain.

298.

It is a grave accusation which admits of no defense.

299.

It is a useless defense which cannot find a fair trial.

300.

The most formidable enemy lies hid in one's own heart.

301.

There are some remedies worse than the disease.

302.

Prudent minds come to settled conclusions.

303.

Repentance for our past deeds is a severe mental punishment.

304.

The anger of the righteous man is the anger most to be dreaded.

305.

Powerful indeed is the empire of habit.

306.

The evil that visits us with a smiling countenance, is the hardest to bear.

307.

The severest affliction is the one which has never been tried.

308.

Frequent marriages give occasion to slander.

309.

A flattering discourse carries its own poison.

310.

Do not take part in the council, unless you are called.

311.

He who stops in mid career is not quite lost.

312.

Better endure an heir, than seek for one.

313.

Under the tears of an heir, there is hidden a smile.

314.

How difficult is it to keep the glory acquired!

315.

How formidable is he who has no fear of death!

316.

Circumstances will oft force a good man to swerve from the right.

317.

Poverty compels men to many untried expedients.

318.

By doing nothing, men learn to do ill.

319.

Amid a multitude of projects, no plan is devised.

320.

When angry, a man has deserted his body.

321.

Men made Fortune a goddess, that misfortune might be certain.

322.

It is easy for men to say one thing, and think another.

323.

We die, as often as we lose a friend.

324.

Man's life is a loan, not a gift.

325.

Necessity is a law that justifies itself.

326.

Success makes some crimes honorable.

327.

An honorable death is better than a disgraceful life.

328.

Honors are soiled when they invest the unworthy.

329.

The well-born should not live base lives.

330.

It is right to spare the guilty, when you thereby shield the innocent.

331.

To submit to necessity involves no disgrace.

332.

Honors adorn the worthy; they are a stigma to the undeserving.

333.

That is the noblest emulation which humanity prompts.

334.

Humility neither falls far, nor heavily.

335.

The people are strongest, where the Laws have most power.

336.

Victory waits upon unity of action.

337.

When the world hates you, see that it have no good reason therefor.

338.

When two do the same thing, it is not the same thing after all.

339.

Indolence never lacks excuse to avoid labor.

340.

A fire can be seen at a great distance, when it gives no heat.

341.

Gold is tried by fire, fortitude by affliction.

342.

It is humane to forgive when the forgiven blushes at the kindness.

343.

Pardon the offense of others, but never your own.

344.

The sinner's judgment began the day that he sinned.

345.

Would you have a great empire? Rule over yourself.

346.

The sinner who repented *after* the offense, was a little imprudent.

347.

It is not wrong to harm him, who has done wrong to you. *

---

* This is no better than the Old Testament maxim: "A tooth for a *tooth, and an eye for an eye."—Trans.*

348.

Authority has less influence than beauty, where love is concerned.

349.

When we yield to love, we are aiding to our own haven.

350.

Love's anger is always hypocritical.

351.

A laugh at the unfortunate is a wrong done him.

352.

Committed against the unfortunate, injustice is powerful.

353.

Life itself is an insult to the wretched.

354.

That life is most pleasant which is passed in ignorance.

355.

Avarice is kind to no one, and most cruel toward itself.

356.

Audacity is every thing, when the danger is critical.

357.

A cock has great influence on his own dung-hill.

358.

Any one can hold the helm, when the sea is calm.

359.

When the offense is a disgrace, it is a double sin to commit it.

360.

Pain and pleasure vie with each other in love.

361.

The madness of love is ever delightful.

362.

Haste is a crime, when the judge is deliberating.

363.

To be not too sanguine of our conclusions, is one half of wisdom.

364.

Indolence consists in seeking excuses from labor.

365.

When labor is shunned, laziness shows its face.

366.

Innocence is the solace of the wretched.

367.

The subordinate perceives all the failings of his superior.

368.

It is a weak mind that cannot bear the possession of riches.

369.

A truly noble nature cannot be insulted.

370.

To request an unworthy action offends a manly spirit.

371.

A noble soul has no ear for unjust reproaches.

372.

Those are unacceptable favors that carry terror to the recipient.

373.

Earth produces no viler creature than an ingrate.

374.

One ingrate is a curse to the whole world of unfortunates.

375.

No prayers reach the heart of an enemy.

376.

No tears are shed, when an enemy dies.

377.

However humble your enemy, it is wise to fear him.

378.

To avenge one's self on an enemy, is to receive a second life.

379.

A neighbor is apt to look on our affairs with an evil eye.

380.

Slander is more injurious than open violence.

381.

The ear bears an injury better than the eye.

382.

It is easier to do an injury than to bear one.

383.

To forget the wrongs you receive, is to remedy them.

384.

He confers a double favor on the needy, who gives in season.

385.

Poverty needs little; avarice every thing.

386.

The madman thinks the rest of the world crazy.

387.

Cupidity in the midst of riches is an armed indigence.

388.

The bow too tensely strung is easily broken.

389.

To do good you should know what good is.

390.

There is more venom than truth in the words of envy.

391.

The rancor of envy is concealed, but is none the less hostile.

392.

To withstand the assaults of envy, you must be either a hero or saint.

393.

It is more agreeable to be envied than pitied.

394.

Crimes are encouraged by overlooking petty offenses.

395.

Detain a man against his will, and you urge him to depart.

396.

Shun an angry man for a moment — your enemy forever.

397.

Anger thinks crime justifiable.

398.

Every word of an angry man conveys a reproach.

399.

When the angry man grows cool, he is angry with himself.

400.

That mortal needs least, who wishes least.

401.

Treat your friend as if he might become an enemy.

402.

Put such confidence in your friend, that he shall find no cause to become an enemy.

403.

Where one has led the way, another may follow.

404.

Every excellence continues unknown, which fame does not blaze abroad.

405.

Pleasant to see, is the stain from the blood of an enemy.

406.

No pleasure endures unseasoned by variety.

407.

The judge is condemned, when the criminal is acquitted.

408.

The right is ever beyond the reach of the wrong

409.

The magistrate should hear both right and wrong side.

410.

The gods give man one good, as an offset to two ills.

411.

Labor is the best of condiments for youth's food.

412.

When injured, our enemy's anguish assuages our own.

413.

The error repeated is a fault.

414.

Libertinage and moral worth never go together.

415.

When you bestow favors on a multitude, many will be thrown away for a single one that goes to the right place.

416.

When vice is approved, it will soon become intolerable.

417.

Unless a man add to his glory, he loses what he has.

418.

The guilty dread the law, the innocent fear fortune.

419.

Anger is apt to forget the existence of law.

420.

Hares can gambol over the body of a dead lion

421.

It is a universal law which ordains birth and death.

422.

Caprice is the mark of a frivolous spirit.

423.

Frivolity, not sobriety, affects intemperate enjoyment.

424.

The Law keeps her eye on the angry man, when he does not see the Law.

425.

When the lion is dead, even puppies can bite him.

426.

He who chases two hares will catch neither.

427.

Fortune is fickle, and speedily asks back her favors.

428.

The love of pleasure is universal, though every face does not show it.

429.

When you assail truth, you may give loose reins to your tongue.

430.

Dignities heaped on the undeserving, are a badge of disgrace.

431.

A slanderous tongue is the sign of a bad heart.

432.

He who lives in solitude, may make his own laws.

433.

A long life makes acquaintance with a thousand ills.

434.

Far distant seems the object when desire is ardent.

435.

Profits in trade can be made only by another's loss.

436.

Nature finds us better heirs than our testaments.

437.

The greater our strength, the less we know of the power of misfortune.

438.

In the art of praying, necessity is the best of teachers.

439.

Practice is the best of all instructors.

440.

A great fortune sits gracefully on a great man.

441.

A noble spirit finds a cure for injustice in forgetting it.

442.

Mighty rivers may easily be leaped at their source.

443.

Excessive indignation is sometimes evidence of a great crime.

444.

It is a bad cause that takes refuge in the lenity of the judge.

445.

Hard to bear is the poverty which follows [a bad use of] riches.

446.

It is a bad medicine that exhausts the powers of nature.

447.

It is a sorry pleasure which is dispensed at the pleasure of another.

448.

A miserable death is an insult from destiny.

449.

Dispositions naturally bad have little need of a teacher.

450.

When you merely wish for what is disgraceful, you violate decorum.

451.

It is bad management when we suffer fortune to be our guide.

452.

The physician were ill, if no one else were ill.

53.

Supreme power may be lost by an abuse of power.

454.

The patient treats his case badly when he makes the physician his heir.

455.

He must have lived ill, who knows not how to die well.

456.

By showing how an evil can be done, you make it worse.

457.

They live ill who expect to live always.

458.

Malevolence keeps its teeth hidden.

459.

He who is bent on doing evil, can never want occasion.

460.

An envious disposition feeds upon itself.

461.

It is a sad victory which brings repentance in the hour of triumph.

462.

The ungrateful above all others, teach us severity and distrust.

463.

One man's wickedness may easily become all men's curse.

464.

Depravity pretends to goodness, that it may be worse than before.

465.

You may spare a bad man, if a good one must die with him.

466.

Woman is man's superior in cunning.

467.

Never find your delight in another's misfortune.

468.

Evil counsels are the greatest curse to him who gives them.

469.

It is a bad plan that admits of no modification.

470.

He is a bad servant who teaches his master.

471.

The more reconciled, the worse the thoughts of a bad heart.

472.

An evil mind cannot counsel well for itself.

473.

The vicious are most to be feared, when they pretend to be good.

474.

He should be called bad, who is good only for selfish ends.

475.

When the ill-inclined cannot do mischief, they still dream of it.

476.

He will become wicked himself, who feasts with the wicked.

477.

In the punishment of the wicked, there is safety for the good.

478.

When the case is clear, it pronounces judgment for itself.

479.

A gentle course is a safe one, but it invites oppression.

480.

When you are at sea, keep clear of the land.

481.

Equanimity is calamity's medicine.

482.

Oblivion is the only remedy for wretchedness.

483.

Intemperance is the physician's provider.

484.

It is better to have a little than nothing.

485.

A mistress is an occasion of dishonor.

486.

Fear cannot restrain, when pleasure invites.

487.

Fear old age, for it does not come without company.

488.

That must be always guarded, which you would keep safely.

489.

Fear, and not kindness, restrains the vicious.

490.

There is poor sleeping with care for a bedfellow.

491.

The less Fortune has given, the less can she take away.

492.

The prompter the refusal, the less the disappointment.

493.

The master who fears his slave, is the greater slave.

494.

The good man can be called miserable, but he is not so.

495.

Wretched the pleasure which is alloyed with a sense of danger.

496.

Unhappy he who must pass life in the midst of perils.

497.

To live free from danger is to know nothing of misery.

498.

A beneficent citizen is a blessing to his country.

499.

It is an unhappy lot which finds no enemies.

500.

It is an unhappy lot which an enemy does not envy.

501.

To depend on another's nod for a livelihood, is a sad destiny.

502.

Compulsory silence is intolerable when one burns to speak freely.

503.

Methinks you are unhappy, if you never have been so.

504.

There is diligence in mature deliberation.

505.

Delay is always vexatious, but it is wisdom's opportunity.

506.

Understand your friend's character, but do not hate it.

507.

An orator's life is more convincing than his eloquence.

508.

Happy the man who dies before he prays for death.

509.

You must die, but not as often as you may have wished.

510.

There is no mortal whom sorrow cannot reach.

511.

The fear of death is more to be dreaded than death itself.

512.

When you have learned to despise death, you will have overco. every terror.

513.

Every thing which has birth, must pay tribute to death.

514.

A woman's tear is spite's seasoning.

515.

There are many displeased when a woman weds many.

516.

A woman's solitary thoughts are her worst ones.

517.

You will find a great many things before you find a good man.

518.

Power gains power by a multitude of pardons.

519.

He threatens many, who does injustice to one.

520.

Seek to please many, and you seek a failure.

521.

The death of a good man is a public calamity.

522.

He whom many fear, has himself many to fear.

523.

Gifts, and not tears, soften the heart of a courtesan.

524.

A rolling stone gathers no moss.

525.

When her anger is kindled by injustice, goodness changes her form.

526.

When a vile man does right, he conceals his true character.

527.

Let not your benevolence extend beyond your means.

528.

Never promise more than you can perform.

529.

Begin nothing, the accomplishment of which you will repent.

530.

No one can escape death or love.

531.

Man has no enduring lease of life or fortune.

532.

Necessity may force from men whatever she wishes.

533.

Necessity imposes laws, but does not receive them.

534.

Want renders a needy man a liar.

535.

On what a firm foundation rests the empire of necessity.

536.

In vain may we look for that which fate conceals.

537.

Necessity takes what she wishes by force, if not voluntarily yielded.

538.

We should bear our destiny, not weep over it.

539.

Necessity can turn any weapon to advantage.

540.

A wise man never refuses any thing to necessity.

541.

Frugality is a remedy for indigence.

542.

Avarice never lacks a reason for refusing a favor.

543.

We refuse ourselves [the thing desired], when we ask what can not be had.

544.

It is natural not to credit [the possibility of] great crimes.

545.

No one should be judge in his own cause.

546.

No one dies too soon, whom misery slays.

547.

No one is so poor during life, as at birth.

548.

Be the first to laugh at your own blunder, and no one will laugh at you.

549.

Fear never advanced any man to the highest standing.

550.

Depravity is its own greatest punishment.

551.

When the bad imitate the good, there is no knowing what mischief is intended.

552.

He who is always unlucky, had better do nothing.

553.

Necessity knows no law except to conquer.

554.

Fortune takes nothing away but her own gifts.

555.

There is nothing more wretched than a mind conscious of its own wickedness.

556.

Our most poignant reflections arise from shame for past acts.

557.

Nothing can be done at once hastily and prudently.

558.

It is pleasant to do a favor for him who does not ask it.

559.

We desire nothing so much as what we ought not to have.

560.

There is nothing which the lapse of time will not either extinguish or improve.

561.

There is no fruit which is not bitter before it is ripe.

562.

The eyes are not responsible when the mind does the seeing.

563.

To be deprived of all capacity for action, is to be at once alive and dead.

564.

Consider nothing which is liable to change a permanent possession.

565.

Consider nothing beneath your notice which may contribute to your safety.

566.

There is no more shameful sight, than an old man commencing life.

567.

Too much candor is easily duped.

568.

The truth is lost when there is too much contention about it.

569.

If there is no evil in death, there is too much good in it.

570.

Stretch the cord too tightly, and it will be likely to break.

571.

It is only the ignorant who despise education.

572.

It is vain to be the pupil of a sage if you have no brains yourself.

573.

He can best avoid a snare who knows how to set one.

574.

Not to punish offenses, is to encourage depravity.

575.

Guilty men beg, the innocent are indignant.

576.

The ready apologist of guilt may be himself suspected.

577.

A resolute spirit is not cast down by a single misfortune.

578.

To abstain from doing injury when you have the power to do it, deserves the greatest praise.

579.

Do not despise the lowest steps in the ascent to greatness.

580.

Don't turn back when you are just at the goal.

581.

It is not every question that deserves an answer.

582.

He is not likely to perish in the ruins who trembles at a crack in the wall.

583.

To control a man against his will, is not to correct him, but injure him.

584.

No man is happy who does not think himself so.

585.

It is not goodness to be barely better than the worst are.

586.

No scar is dishonorable which is a mark of our courage.

587.

There can never be an overplus of honorable actions.

588.

The anguish thoroughly allayed should not be rudely awakened.

589.

That is not very small which is barely less than the greatest.

590.

That is not yours which fortune made yours.

591.

It is hard to think the habitually innocent guilty of crime.

592

You will find it difficult to be sole guardian over that which multitudes covet.

593.

Never thrust your own sickle into another's corn.

594.

A prompt refusal is sometimes no slight service.

595.

Courage cannot be cast down by adversity.

596.

You cannot put the same shoe on every foot.

597.

Do not suppose every thing will come to pass as you have arranged for it.

598.

He bids fair to grow wise, who has discovered that he is not so.

599.

Don't consider how many you can please, but whom.

600.

Good fortune does not always lend a ready ear.

601.

It is not safe to indulge in a play of wits with kings.

602.

It is never too late to take the road to rectitude.

603.

To yield to our friends is not to be overcome, but to conquer.

604.

There is no pleasure which continued enjoyment cannot render disgusting.

605.

Misfortune is most men's greatest punishment.

606.

Of all men, the bad man's fellow can be most readily found.

607.

Never thrust upon another the burden you cannot carry yourself.

608.

Pity is well spoken of in all lands.

609.

There is no great evil which does not bring with it some advantage.

610.

Consider that there is no place without a [hidden] witness.

611

No wise man has ever put faith in a traitor.

612.

Our greatest gains are made by sparing what we possess [i. e., by economy].

613.

Crimes are most easily concealed in the midst of a crowd.

614.

He is never happy whose thoughts always run with his fears.

615.

No danger incurred, no danger repelled.

616.

You can never give enough to satisfy unlawful expectations.

617.

A guilty conscience never feels secure.

618.

Where a fire has long burned there is always some smoke.

619.

The worst danger is that which is concealed.

620.

Who knows how great are the secret pangs of conscience?

621.

How long is life to the wretched, how short for the happy!

622.

The kind attentions of the wife, speedily gender disgust for the concubine.

623.

Opportunities are easily lost, with difficulty found.

624.

It is hard to recover the lost opportunity.

625.

It is an honorable death that delivers from an ignominious servitude.

626.

When the performer is concealed, we are indifferent to the music.

627.

Put more confidence in your eyes than your ears.

628.

I dislike a precocious talent in little boys.

629.

He is a despicable sage whose wisdom does not profit himself.

630.

Some enmities conceal themselves beneath a mask, some under a kiss.

631.

Every vicious act has its excuse ever ready.

632.

A cheerful obedience is universal, when the worthy bear rule.

633.

Every day should be passed as if it were to be our last.

634.

Every fascinating pleasure is an injurious pleasure.

635.

There should be no disagreement between our lives and our doctrines.

636.

Be at war with men's vices, at peace with themselves.

637.

Craft, and not sorrow, is seen in a hypocrite's tears.

638.

An angry father is most cruel toward himself.

639.

To know how to obey is as honorable as to rule.

640.

Familiarity breeds contempt.

641.

Easy is the intercourse of equals with equals.

642.

We find something of the favor sought in a graceful refusal.

643.

A prompt denial is something toward the favor requested.

644.

Hunger goes with stinted supplies, disgust attends on abundance.

645.

By tolerating many abuses, we encourage the assaults of such as we cannot tolerate.

646.

Patience and fortitude create their own happiness.

647.

Patience in adversity is by no means felicity.

648.

Patience reveals the soul's hidden riches.

649.

Any land is your country where you can live happy.

650.

There are few to appreciate what God gives to all.

651.

A few men's depravity is all men's calamity.

652.

There are few unwilling to sin, none without knowledge thereof.

653.

It is right to wish your friend's fault concealed.

654.

You do well to consider your friend's error your own.

655.

He who promptly corrects, makes his error the less.

656.

Money alone sets all the world in motion.

657.

Be your money's master, not its slave.

658.

The worse the precepts, the more easy for youth to learn.

659.

Mute grief feels a keener pang than that which cries aloud.

660.

Always study to secure your permanent peace.

661.

An end to our gettings is the only end to our losses.

662.

The greater will be lost, if the less is not saved.

663.

A gift is a loss, where gratitude is not the receiver.

664.

It is the soul, not the body, that makes an enduring marriage.

665.

To know the hour of death is to die every moment.

666.

A happy man is he who obtains his wishes easily.

667.

To take refuge with an inferior, is to betray one's self.

668.

The timid man sees dangers that do not exist.

669.

He who dares danger, triumphs over it before it reaches him.

670.

He who exercises clemency gains a victory for all time.

671.

No one can long sustain a false character.

672.

He invites danger who indulges in anger.

673.

He who has plenty of pepper, will pepper his cabbage.

674.

You should go to a pear tree for pears, not to an elm.

675.

It is a very hard undertaking to seek to please every body.

676.

Friends delight in the dishes which cordiality seasons.

677.

Most men are good through fear, not through a love of goodness.

678.

God generally finds a way for like to meet like.

679.

Fortune shields more people than she secures.

680.

Harken rather to your conscience than to opinion.

681.

It is easier to submit to punishment than to injustice.

682.

To live in misery and destitution is worse than punishment.

683.

Slander is a greater outrage than personal violence.

684.

Punishment creeps upon wickedness secretly in order to crush it.

685.

The less the pain, the lighter the punishment.

686.

Punishment tarries for vice, but never passes it by.

687.

Whoever is useful to his country, is the people's property.

688.

The memory of great misfortunes suffered, is itself a misfortune.

689.

A merciful man in power is a public blessing.

690.

To get angry with power, is to invite danger on one's own head.

691.

Freedom alone is the source of noble action.

692.

Prosperity has no power over adversity.

693.

He whose vengeance is sated in his absence, is ever present with his victim.

694.

Methinks it is better to be envied than pitied.

695.

It is deception to refuse first, and afterward perform.

696.

Gratitude for a favor is sufficient interest therefor.

697.

To do wrong for a master is a meritorious act.

698.

The pain which kills pain, is as good as a medicine.

699.

When you have good materials, employ good workmen.

700.

The judge who ignores a good man's offenses, wipes them out.

701.

A good reputation is a good man's noblest inheritance.

702.

He who does a kindness to the deserving, shares it with him.

703.

A worthy freedman is a son acquired without the aid of nature.

704.

Unhappy he, who cannot do the good that he would.

705.

He benefits who will not injure when he can.

706.

It is an unjust sentence which extends the deserved penalty too far.

707.

He who is eager to condemn, takes delight in condemning.

708.

A hasty verdict betrays a desire to find a crime committed.

709.

We should provide in peace what we need in war.

710.

Wit itself is folly in a sage.

711.

Lost modesty never returns to grace the loser.

712.

Modesty may be born, it never can be taught.

713.

He will yield to fear, who has no regard for honor.

714.

The nurselings of avarice have but a short time to stay.

715.

God looks at the clean hands, not the full ones.

716.

You need not seek twice for the rose already withered.

717.

In being modest there is a slight touch of servility.

718.

He who violates another's honor loses his own.

719.

The friendship that can come to an end, never really began.

720.

What it is right to do, should be done at the right time.

721.

Do not seek for that which you would be ashamed to find.

722.

The woman too anxious to seem fair, cannot say No.

723.

Look for a tough wedge for a tough log.

724.

How oppressive is the weight of an evil conscience!

725.

How happy the life unembarassed by the cares of business!

726.

How great a matter is it to deserve praise, though we do not receive it!

727.

How vile is he who charges his own offenses upon others!

728.

How much to be pitied is he, who has no pity!

729.

How unhappy is he who cannot forgive himself!

730.

How poor the assistance which injures while it aids!

731.

How hard it is to be compelled to regret our good deeds!

732.

Sad is it to be forced to ruin him whom you would save.

733.

It is a great loss to lose that which few possess.

734.

Unhappy fate, to long for death and be unable to find it.

735.

It is a great grievance when the evil which is past returns again.

736.

How hard is it when accident triumphs over design!

737.

It is a bitter fate when one's defenders become his jailors.

738.

How bootless the kindness which is followed by no good result!

739.

How much must he repent of who lives a long life!

740.

How often must he ask for pardon who has refused it when asked!

741.

How timid is he who stands in terror of poverty!

742.

The bitterness of the admonition never does harm.

743.

Consider the useful agreeable, even though if were not.

744.

When our incense falls short, we offer salt cakes.

745.

It is wrong even to complain of him whom you love.

746.

He whom public opinion has once degraded, rarely recovers his former standing.

747.

If you delight in the society of the vicious, you are vicious yourself.

748.

He who can best play the hypocrite, can soonest injure his enemy.

749.

How shall we treat with those who say one thing, and mean another?

750.

Pardon one offense, and you encourage the commission of many more.

751.

The debtor does not like the sight of his creditor's door.

752.

He who yields a prudent obedience, exercises a partial control.

753.

He makes many offenders, who is reluctant to punish.

754.

He lessens the favor conferred, who waits to be asked.

755.

He is suspected on all matters, who makes a failure in one.

756.

He who hesitates to take the right course, deliberates to no purpose.

757.

A slave against his will is wretched, but none the less a slave.

758.

He who adheres to his oath will come out where he wishes.

759.

They who plow the sea do not carry the winds in their hands.

760.

He who guards against calamities rarely meets them.

761.

It is no vice to keep a vice out of sight.

762.

He who can play the fool at pleasure can be wise if he will.

763.

He who has the power to injure is feared in his absence.

764.

He who has the power to harm is dreaded when he does not intend harm.

765.

He who can transfer his love [to a new object] can subdue it.

766.

It is the height of eloquence to speak in the defense of the innocent.

767.

He gets through too late who goes too fast.

768.

He who coaxes after he is hurt is prudent out of time.

769.

He who praises himself will speedily find a censor.

770.

He who accuses himself rarely wants good reason for it.

771.

He who lives only for himself is truly dead to others.

772.

He who fears his friend teaches his friend to fear him.

773.

He who distrusts his friend knows not the meaning of the word.

774.

He who dreads all manner of snares will fall into none.

775.

He who comes to injure intended the evil before he set out.

776

Give to the good and a share returns to yourself.

777.

In every enterprise consider where you would come out.

778.

Virtue's deeds are glory's deeds.

779.

The honors for which we are indebted to fortune, quickly lose their luster.

780.

It takes a long time to bring excellence to maturity.

781.

The highest condition takes its rise in the lowest.

782.

He who has learned how to injure, recollects the lesson when occasion offers.

783.

You should tell no one what you wish no one to know.

784.

What is it to practice benevolence? It is to imitate the Deity.

785.

It matters not what you are thought to be, but what you are.

786.

No one knows what he can do till he tries.

787.

What do you need of money if you cannot use it?

788.

The defect which one period of life fastens upon us, another will remove.

789.

Some men are bitter enemies and poor friends.

790.

They pass peaceful lives who ignore *mine* and *thine.*

791.

Who would recognise the unhappy if grief had no language?

792.

Who is a poor man? He who thinks himself rich.

793.

Who has the greatest possessions? He who wants least.

794.

What you blame in others as a fault, you should not be guilty of yourself.

795.

Neglect a danger and it will some time take you by surprise.

796.

The wise man guards against future evils as if they were present.

797.

What it is disgraceful to do, think it no honor to speak of.

798.

That which you thought to run away from, will often meet you face to face.

799.

It is foolish to hoard, when you know not for whom you do it.

800.

It is the height of folly to blame without knowledge.

801.

We can lament for that which is lost, but we cannot get it back.

802.

What we admire, we never cease commending to ourselves.

803.

That does not always please us which is always within reach.

804.

The world thinks that old age always speaks wisely.

805.

What we fear comes to pass more speedily than what we hope.

806.

It matters not with what purpose you do it, if the act itself be bad.

807.

That which is hardly brought to pass hardly gives pleasure.

808.

Passion dreams of what it desires, not of what is becoming.

809.

He can have what he wishes who wishes just enough.

810.

When the soul rules over itself its empire is lasting.

811.

Even the Milesians were once valiant.

812.

Calamity can easily discover whomsoever she seeks.

813.

A man has as many enemies in his own house as he has slaves.

814.

He is condemned every day who stands in daily fear of condemnation.

815.

The next day is never so good as the day before.

816.

When you are in love you are not wise; or, when you are wise you are not in love.

817.

When you give to avarice you invite an injury.

818.

When you forgive an enemy you gain many friends.

819.

When a wise man conquers himself, his conquest is worth something.

820.

* When vice is profitable, he errs who does right.

821.

A frog would leap from a throne of gold into a puddle.

822.

It is robbery to receive a favor which you cannot return.

823.

It is robbing, not asking, when you take from a man against his will.

824.

That must be rare which you desire to be a long time precious.

825.

He is truly wise who gains wisdom from another's mishap.

826.

Youth should be governed by reason, not by force.

---

* This maxim is at once the climax of worldly wisdom and genuine folly, and was probably put by Syrus in the mouth of some unscrupulous scoundrel personated in a mime.

827.

Good health and good sense are two of life's greatest blessings.

828.

He who gives to each man his due, pays a debt and loses nothing himself.

829.

It matters not how long you live but how well.

830.

Don't turn back when you are just at the goal.

831.

He who imposes his own talk on the circle, does not converse; he plays the master.

832.

Fortune tosses off her wheel the destinies of kings.

833.

Delay profits nothing but a hasty temper.

834.

We get rid of bitter bile with bitter medicines.

835.

*It is vain to look for a defense against lightning.

836.

It is more tolerable to be refused than deceived.

837.

No good man ever grew rich all at once.

838.

Forgetfulness is our only relief against losses.

839.

Prosperity is ever providing itself with anxieties.

---

* Truisms in matters touching human progress in one age, become falsehoods in another. Syrus would not have said this, had he been a cotemporary of Franklin.

840.

The greater our good fortune, the more likely to fail us.

841.

Anger stops at nothing.

842.

Accused innocence fears fate, not the witnesses.

843.

It is not a hard lot to be obliged to return to the state whence we came.

844.

I should not please to be king, if I must therefore be pleased to be cruel.

845.

The hour of triumph loves no co-partnership.

846.

You can obey a request much better than a command.

847.

* Every thing is worth what its purchaser will pay for it.

848.

Give your friend cause to blush, and you will be likely to lose him.

849.

Repeated pardons encourage offenses.

850.

To prefer a request smacks of servility to a noble spirit.

851.

You would not sin so often if you knew some things of which you are ignorant.

This saying is equivalent to the maxim current in our day: *a thing is worth what it will fetch.* There can be no millenium for civilized man till this maxim has ceased to be true, and a thing becomes worth the labor it cost to produce it.

852.

The eyes and ears of the mob are often false witnesses.

853.

You must buy a bushel of salt [with cash down] before you get credit.

854.

It is right to injure a man to save his life.

855.

There is no more sacred duty than to remember to whom you owe yourself.

856.

When the wise man thinks, he arms himself against the assaults of the whole world.

857.

The sage briefly refuses your request by his silence.

858.

Folly is very often wisdom's companion.

859.

Useful, and not multifarious knowledge, is widom.

860.

Vain is that wisdom which does not profit the possessor.

861.

You are eloquent enough if truth speaks through you.

862.

Happy he who can die when he wishes.

863.

It is enough to vanquish an enemy; more than enough to ruin him.

864.

It is better to learn late than never.

865.

Better be ignorant of a matter than half know it.

866.

Better use medicines at the outset, than at the last moment.

867.

The sons of the blacksmith are not frightened at sparks.

868.

The judge is condemned when he punishes the innocent.

869.

The angry think their power greater than it is.

870.

Speak well of your friend in public, admonish him in secret.

871.

Credit is poverty's good fortune.

872.

Prosperity makes friends, adversity tries them.

873.

The nurse's grief is almost as great as the mother's.

874.

Sedition among the citizens is the enemy's opportunity.

875.

He who has been once a criminal always passes for such.

876.

Kindness of heart is always happy.

877.

Human prudence ever fails when there is most need of it.

878.

The wise man avoids evil by anticipating it.

879.

Always shun whatever may make you angry.

880.

Fear always comes back to curse its authors.

881.

It is late to be devising expedients when the danger is at hand.

882.

Bright faculties are the source of wisdom, not length of years.

883.

It is late to guard against evil, when it has already come.

884.

If you would fear nothing, fear every thing.

885.

If you are a mariner, let landsmen's business alone.

886.

There will always be some to hate you, if you love yourself.

887.

Vice is constrained to be its own curse.

888.

To overthrow law, is to destroy our greatest protection.

889.

He punishes himself who repents of his deeds.

890.

He is the most hostile of enemies whose friendship is unreal.

891.

The greatest of empires, is the empire over one's self.

892.

The probity which is only assumed, is depravity doubly distilled.

893.

Guilt's assistant is guilt's participant.

894.

To have the universe bear one company, would be a great consolation in death.

895.

In critical junctures, temerity is wont to take the place of prudence.

896.

An hour sometimes restores us the sum of many years losses.

897.

Glory is apt to follow when industry has prepared the road.

898.

Our lives are apt to be meaner than our births.

899.

There is hope of improvement so long as a man is alive to shame.

900.

Hope is the solace of poverty, money of avarice, death of misery.

901.

The sight of a thorn is pleasant when there is a rose by its side.

902.

Fools stand in dread of fortune, wise men bear it.

903.

It is folly to censure him whom all the world adores.

904.

Prosperity sometimes exhibits a little folly.

905.

Only fools commit the error which might have been avoided.

906.

It is folly to take the uncertain for the certain.

907.

It is foolish to complain of the misfortunes which have come to pass through your own fault.

908.

It is folly to dread what cannot be avoided.

909.

It is folly to take vengeance on another to your own injury.

910.

It is folly to punish your neighbour by fire when you live next door.

911.

Whom fortune wishes to destroy, she first makes mad.

912.

It is folly for him to rule over others who cannot govern himself.

913.

He is a fool who envies the happiness of the proud.

914.

Let a fool hold his tongue, and he will pass for a sage.

915.

He preserves his family's property who does not waste his own.

916.

Benevolence tries persuasion first, and then severer measures.

917.

A pleasant life this, if you know nothing; for ignorance is a painless evil.

918.

The stolen ox sometimes puts his head out of the stall.

919.

A lax government can not maintain its authority

920.

A boastful prosperity will prepare its own fall.

921.

He favors the enemy who does not spare his own soldiers.

922.

An ultra right is generally an ultra wrong.

923.

The buyers of jewelry always suspect the quality of such ware.

924.

Innocence always follows the guidance of its own light.

925.

Suspicion of the worthy is a secret injustice done them.

926.

We rarely incur danger by silence.

927.

Avarice is as destitute of what it has, as what it has not.

928.

Suspicion begets suspicion.

929.

A suspicious mind distrusts the whole world.

930.

He knows not when to be silent, who knows not when to speak.

931.

Taciturnity is the dunce's wisdom.

932.

As long as man is ignorant, so long he should be a learner.

933.

He is much to be dreaded who stands in dread of poverty.

934.

Timidity styles itself caution; stinginess frugality.

935.

Sweet is the grievance when pleasure defers to profit.

936.

* Do not water your neighbor's fields when your own are parched.

---

* That is, do not be too anxious for the souls of the heathen in India so long as there is no provision made for the heathen in Virginia.

937.

It is a disgraceful indigence which springs from extravagance.

938.

It is a disgraceful loss which is chargeable to negligence.

939.

When one man is protected [by law] all men are safe.

940.

The highest safety is to fear nought but the Almighty.

941.

The poor man is ruined as soon as he begins to ape the rich.

942.

When you purchase another's property, you must part with some of your own.

943.

Where destiny blunders, human prudence will not avail.

944.

When innocence trembles, it condemns the judge.

945.

Where the accuser is the judge, power rules and not law.

946.

When liberty has fallen, no one dares to open his mouth.

947.

The greater your joys, the greater your occasion for fear.

948.

When every body is guilty, the prayer for relief will avail little.

949.

When life is a continual terror, death is a blessing.

950.

When the elder do wrong, the younger learn the lesson.

951

When caution keeps watch, naught comes to pass to be dreaded.

952.

Where reverence dwells, there faith is ever kept.

953.

The wounds of the soul should be cured before those of the body.

954.

A single day executes the punishment, many prepared the way for it.

955.

One will agree with you sooner than many.

956.

It is right that one should perish that many may be saved.

957.

We should use our friends while we have plenty of them.

958.

The commander should foresee every contingency.

959.

Even to be hung one should choose a fine tree.

960.

Either be silent, or say something better than silence.

961.

Penitence follows hasty decisions.

962.

The importance of every word depends on the sense you give it.

963.

Why do we not hear the truth? Because we don't speak it.

964.

A lie is truth, when told for one's safety.

965.

By tolerating an inveterate wrong, you invite a new one.

966.

Vices often have a close relationship to virtues.

967.

It is of advantage to be conquered when our own victory would be a loss.

968.

You need not hang up the ivy branch over the wine that will sel .

969.

The sound of a harp will not stay the flight of a fugitive.

970.

A good man should not know how to do an injury.

971.

You can accomplish by kindness what you can not by force.

972.

No one can honorably refuse to love virtue.

973.

False modesty is an embarrassment to every virtue.

974.

It is better to trust virtue than fortune.

975.

Labor rejoices when it sees the rewards of virtue.

976.

The semblance of courage gains a part of every victory.

977.

It is nature, not his standing, that makes the good man.

978.

Do not take a bad man for your companion on a journey.

979.

Would you be known by every body? Then you know nobody.

980.

Life and reputation travel on with equal pace.

981.

A life of leisure is a kingdom with less care [than a kingdom requires].

982.

Fortune is mistress of life, and not wisdom.

983.

Conceal your opulence if you would avoid envy.

984.

Vices grown inveterate are hard to correct.

985.

Flattery was once a vice, now it is the fashion.

986.

Every vice has its excuse ready.

987.

Pride is prosperity's common vice.

988.

Unchastity resides in the will, not in the body.

989.

The sweetest pleasure arises from difficulties overcome.

990.

There is more of fear than delight in a secret pleasure.

991.

There is a great difference between seeming wise, and being so.

992.

What has been given can be taken away.

993.

The more skilful the gambler, the greater the scoundrel.

994.

Sympathy in benevolence is the strongest of ties.

995.

It is a consolation to the wretched to have companions in misery.

996.

A good conscience never utters mere lip-prayers.

997.

A man of courage never endures an insult; an honorable man never offers one.

998.

Even for wisdom it is a hard matter to bear affliction.

999.

Any opportunity is a good one to him who thirsts for vengeance.

1000.

The life of that man is detested by the citizens, whose death is expected by his friends.

1001.

He is not considered a dupe who understood that he was deceived.

1002.

Call a man an ingrate, and you give him all manner of bad names in one.

1003.

The service is twofold greater when it is promptly rendered.

1004.

The little vices of the great must needs be accounted very great.

1005.

It is an advantage not to possess that which you must hold against your will.

1006.

Disgrace is honorable when you die in a good cause.

1007.

Cruel punishments do no honor to the king's majesty.

1008.

The exile without a home, is a dead man without sepulture.

1009.

Anger would inflict punishment on another; meanwhile, it tortures itself.

1010.

The happy man is not he who seems thus to others, but who seems thus to himself.

1011.

You may despair of quiet, if you manage the affairs of women.

1012.

Error and repentance are the attendants on hasty decisions.

1013.

He who conquers his passions is a man of more nerve than he who subdues the enemy.

1014.

In vain may you ask back your youth when old age has come on.

1015.

The thunderbolt is forged when anger and power meet together.

1016.

He finds assistance in adversity who renders services in prosperity.

1017.

How terrible is that anguish which can find no voice amid tortures!

1018.

How grievous to suffer at the hand of him of whom you dare not complain!

1019.

It is a bitter dose to be taught obedience after you have learned to rule.

1020.

How many causes for repentance do we find during a long life!

1021.

Mercy to the afflicted is a [prudent] remembrance of one's self.

1022.

We have one opinion of ourselves, and another of our neighbor.

1023.

A single hour may often compensate for the losses of ten years.

1024.

He who makes shipwreck a second time does wrong to accuse Neptune.

1025.

None but the innocent in the midst of danger hope for good.

1026.

It is harder to judge between friends than enemies.

1027.

He who subdues his temper vanquishes his greatest enemy.

1028.

Call yourself happy, and you invite [the visits of] misfortune.

1029.

Fear the envy of your friends more than the snares of your enemies.

1030.

Malice swallows the greater part of its own venom.

1031.

There is the greatest danger in guarding what the multitude covet.

1032.

I am not your friend unless I share in your fortunes.

1033.

Death is a blessing to infancy, bitter for youth, too tardy for old age.

1034.

We simply rob ourselves when we make presents to the dead.

1035.

A single instant brings much to pass that no one dreams of.

1036.

Great hatred can be concealed in the countenance, and much in a kiss.

1037.

Verily he abounds in virtues who [merely] loves those of others.

1038.

Count not him among your friends who will retail your privacies to the world.

1039.

Do not be too hasty in accusing, or approving any one.

1040.

You know neither what to hope or fear; you are the sport of a day.

1041.

He can do no harm who has lost the desire to do it.

1042.

* Unless degree is preserved, the first place is safe for no one.

1043.

It is no profit to have learned well, if you neglect to do well.

1044.

Reason avails nothing when passion has the mastery.

1045.

There is no problem so difficult that it can not be solved by investigation.

1046.

You should not lead one life in private and another in public.

1047.

You are not yet happy if the rabble do not make sport of you.

1048.

The house is by no means straightened that holds many friends.

1049.

There is no fortune so good that you can not complain of it.

---

* Take but *degree* away, untune that string,
And, hark, what discord follows! each thing meets
In mere oppugnancy.—*Troilus and Cressida.*

1050.

No where can we die happier then where we have lived happily.

1051.

Reproaches in misfortune are more intolerable than misfortune itself.

1052.

Hatred of evil should constrain you to right, not fear.

1053.

Death ever uncertain gets the start of such as are always beginning to live.

1054.

A service is well rendered when the receiver can remember it.

1055.

It is very well to imitate our ancestors, if they led in the right way.

1056.

The crime of the parent should never be a prejudice to the son.

1057.

Money is a servant if you know how to use it; if not, it is a master.

1058.

When we speak evil of others, we generally condemn ourselves.

1059.

To apply a common fund to our individual uses is the beginning of discord.

1060.

Confession of our faults is the next thing to innocence.

1061.

The later in life evil courses are begun, the more disgraceful they are.

1962.

When you can not restrain a man by kindness, try something else.

1063.

It is an embarrassment to the possessor to have more than he needs.

1064.

What matters it how much you have? There is more which you can not have.

1065.

The same man can rarely say a great deal, and say it to the purpose.

1066.

Much harder is the lot of kings than that of their subjects.

1067.

Not the criminals, but their crimes, it is well to extirpate.

1068.

In our hatred of guilt, it is folly to ruin innocence.

1069.

It is often better to overlook an injury, than avenge it.

1070.

I have often regretted my speech, never my silence.

1071.

You had better please one good man than many bad ones.

1072.

Keep the golden mean, between saying too much and too little.

1073.

Speech is a mirror of the soul; as a man speaks, so is he.

1074.

If you obey against your will, you are a slave; if of your will, you are an assistant.

1075.

Let your life be pleasing to the multitude, and it can not be so to yourself.

1076.

If you gain new friends, don't forget the old ones.

1077.

There is no pain in the wound received in the moment of victory.

1078.

If you would live innocently, seek solitude.

1079.

Avarice is as destitute of what it has, as poverty of what it has not.

1080.

There is as much cruelty in pardoning all, as in pardoning none.

1081.

He lays up his treasure in a sepulchre who makes an old man his heir.

1082.

It is a less evil to be unable to live than not to know how to live.

1083.

A sentence to death is more tolerable than a command to live wickedly.

1084.

An evil conscience is often quiet, but never secure.

1085.

Away from your country, though in the midst of friends, you long to return thither again.

1086.

When the dog is too old you can not get him used to the collar.

1087.

Man's life is short; and therefore an honorable death is his immortality.